Alan Brown's Diary

Frederick L. Wolf

Alan Brown's Diary

DELTA Publishing

You can listen to *Alan Brown's Diary* using the free DELTA Augmented app – you'll also find fun interactive activities!

| Download the free DELTA Augmented app onto your device | Start picture recognition and scan the **contents page** | Download files and use them now or save them for later |

Apple and the Apple logo are trademarks of Apple Inc., registered in the US and other countries. App Store is a service mark of Apple Inc. | Google Play and the Google Play logo are trademarks of Google Inc.

1st edition 1 ⁶ ⁵ ⁴ ³ ² | 2024 23 22 21 20

Delta Publishing, 2019
www.deltapublishing.co.uk

© Ernst Klett Sprachen GmbH, Rotebühlstraße 77, 70178 Stuttgart, 2019

Authors:
Text: Frederick L. Wolf
Annotations and activities: Laura Broadbent

Cover and layout: Andreas Drabarek
Illustrations: Sven Palmowski, Barcelona; Helga Merkle, Zell
Typesetting: Design: Datagroup Int. SRL, Timisoara, Romania
Cover picture: Shutterstock (SnowStock), New York;

Printing and binding: Salzland Druck, Staßfurt, Germany

ISBN 978-3-12-501120-5

Contents

Abbreviations

sb   = somebody
sth = something

Before you start

1. Do you have a diary? What are the good things about writing a diary? And the bad things about it?
2. Here are some things people typically write about in diaries. Make notes about what you would write in each category:

What I did well	What I'm scared of	What I want to do	What I don't want to do
-helped my mum	-Spiders	-homework	-homework

What I like	What I don't like	What I worry about	People I know
-food	-spiders	-/	-fam + friends

3. Read *Alan Brown's Diary* and find out which of these things he writes about. What else does he write about?

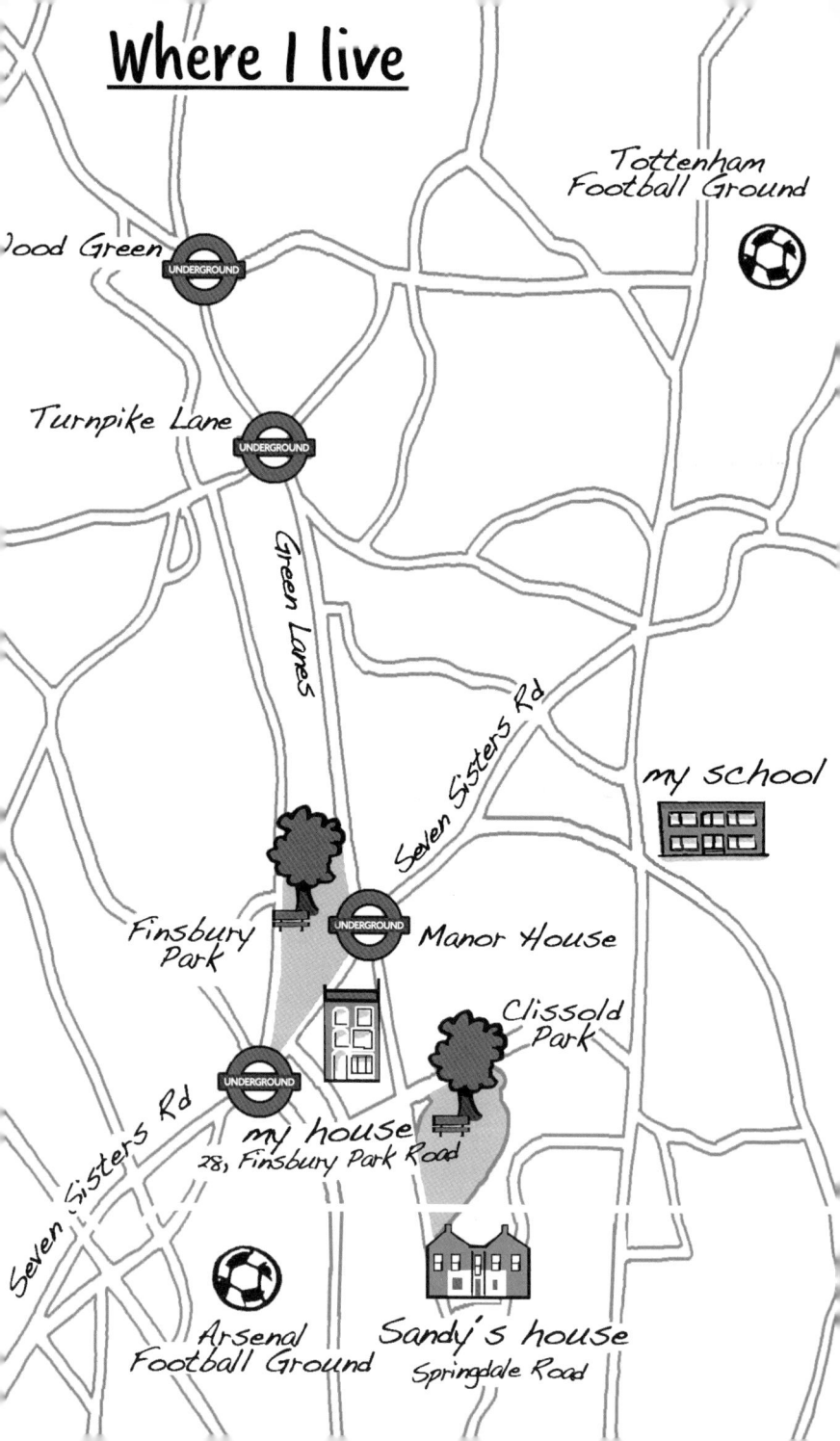

Where I live

Tottenham
Football Ground

Wood Green

UNDERGROUND

Turnpike Lane

UNDERGROUND

Green Lanes

Seven Sisters Rd

my school

Finsbury
Park

UNDERGROUND

Manor House

Clissold
Park

UNDERGROUND

my house
28, Finsbury Park Road

Seven Sisters Rd

Arsenal
Football Ground

Sandy's house
Springdale Road

About me

My name is Alan Brown.
I live at 28, Finsbury Park Road, London N4.
My hobbies are football and pop music.
I'm also interested in girls.
My favourite subjects are Physical Education and Music.
I hate Geography, Maths and French.
My sister is 17 and stupid.
My mother is a housewife.
My father works away from home.

---

9 **stupid** not intelligent, silly – 10 **housewife** a woman who stays at home to look after the house and family

Part I

Monday, September 24th

It was great at school today. There was a new girl in our class. Her name is Sandy and she's from Manchester. She moved to London with her family last weekend. She's fantastic. It's a pity that she doesn't sit next to me. She sits next to Kevin. How can she??? Kevin looks like a monkey.
I haven't talked to Sandy yet, but I'll try tomorrow.

Tuesday, September 25th

I couldn't speak to Sandy because she wasn't at school today. I don't know what happened to her. Perhaps she's ill. I couldn't follow the lessons because I was thinking of Sandy all the time. I hope she will be in school tomorrow.

Wednesday, September 26th

Sandy was there again. Ah! But I haven't spoken to her yet. I wanted to a few times, but I just couldn't do it. She has beautiful hair. I love it. During the Geography lesson the teacher asked me, "What's the capital of Germany?" – I was dreaming of Sandy and her long red hair. It's wonderful. – The teacher shouted, "Alan, wake up! What's the capital of Germany?" I was still dreaming and so I said, "Long red hair." – Everybody was laughing. Only the teacher became very angry and shouted at me again. Mr Johnson shouts too much – I don't think it's good for him.

---

5 **it's a pity** it's sad or disappointing

It's ten o'clock in the evening now, and I'm watching an action
film on TV. My mother has gone out and my sister won't be
home until late. So I have the lounge all to myself. I'm a bit
worried because I haven't learned my French vocabulary for
tomorrow yet. Perhaps I can start when the film is over.

Thursday, September 27th

I was lucky! Our French teacher was ill today. We had
a Biology lesson instead. We talked about insects. I wonder if
insects can fall in love, too.
During the History lesson Brian threw bits of
paper at Sandy all the time. It really made me
angry. After the lesson I told Brian to keep
his fingers off Sandy. Brian only laughed and
showed off his big muscles ...

Friday, September 28th

TGIF!! (Thank God it's Friday!)
At last. I met Sandy in the school cafeteria during lunch break.
I nearly dropped my plate of sausage and chips over her. I'm glad
I didn't because she looked great in her new school uniform.
I asked her, "Do you like it at our school?" She said, "NO!" I tried
hard to smile at her but I think I looked too serious.
Brian said some dirty things about me at the lunch table. If he
goes on like that he will get himself into trouble. My mother went
out again. It's the second night this week that she has stayed out
late. I wonder what she's doing!

---

11 **insect** a very small animal with legs, head and sometimes wings – 12 **to fall in love** to
start loving sb – 15 **to keep your fingers off sb** to not touch sb – 17 **to show off your
muscles** to try to impress sb by showing them how strong you are

I wanted to sleep in today. But the milkman rang the doorbell at seven o'clock. He wanted to tell us that the price of milk had gone up again. Why can't he do it on a school day?
I had a nice dream last night. I dreamed that I was walking hand in hand with Sandy through the streets of Manchester. She looked even more beautiful in jeans and a green top than in her new school uniform.
She told me everything about her life and that she was in love with me. I wanted to tell her that I was in love with her, too.
I wanted to kiss her, but then that stupid milkman rang the doorbell and woke me up. The dream was over.

I stayed in bed until 11 o'clock. When I came into the kitchen Mum was sitting at the kitchen table. Something was wrong. She hadn't brushed her hair and she had no make-up on. She usually puts her make-up on before breakfast. Her glasses were lying on the table and she was crying. She said, "I haven't heard from your father for a week now. I've tried to phone him but nobody answers the phone ..."

Where does Alan's father work?

Why does Alan find it hard to concentrate in class?

3 **milkman** sb who brings milk to your house – 21 **glasses** sth you wear on your face to help you see better

Think about it ...

It's sometimes hard to concentrate in class. What do you think about when you should be listening to the teacher?

I didn't sleep very well. I'm worried about Dad. He's working on an oil rig in the North Sea somewhere east of Scotland. I know that it can be a very hard and dangerous job. You can easily slip and break an arm or a leg or you can fall into the water and die when there's a storm. There could also be a fire or an explosion. There was some kind of small "explosion" in my room. My computer doesn't work anymore. I don't know what's wrong with it.

The most fantastic thing happened to me today. During morning break Sandy asked me to help her with the French homework. I didn't know what to say, I was so surprised. I hope this means I will get a second chance.

Good news from my dad. He phoned us today to tell us that there had been a terrible storm in the North Sea and that they hadn't been able to telephone anybody. Now the storm is over and everything is back to normal. I wonder what life on an oil rig is like. It must be very boring. You can't go anywhere and you see the same people all the time.

I told my mother at breakfast that I want a guitar for Christmas. I want to be a pop star. My mother said that she wanted to talk about this with my father first. That's a good sign.

---

4 **oil rig** small place at sea where people who look for oil live and work – 7 **to slip** to fall

I saw a strange-looking man standing on the corner of the street
when I came home from school. At seven o'clock he was still
standing there.

I tried to write a little poem for Sandy, but I don't think it's good
enough yet. I'll try again over the weekend.
My sister came home with a dog. It looks really funny. It's grey and
white. It has long ears and a big face. It's also quite fat. My sister
likes it because of its beautiful brown eyes. She said that it had run
after her all the way home from the tube station. My mother didn't
want to take the dog in. So we put him up in the garden.

Friday, October 5th

Didn't sleep very well because the dog was
barking in the garden all the time. At four
o'clock in the morning we had to bring
the dog inside because the neighbours
began to shout at it to shut up. My
mother put the dog in the kitchen.
At seven o'clock my mother got up.
She went into the kitchen but the
dog wasn't there. She found it in the
lounge lying on the sofa. There was a funny smell. Mother
became very angry. "The dog must go!", she said. My sister started
crying. At eight o'clock my sister and the dog left the house.

---

1 **strange-looking man** a man who doesn't look normal – 8 **poem** piece of spoken artistic
work. Poems often rhyme. – 13 **tube station** underground train stop in London – 23 **to
shut up** to stop speaking – 28 **smell** you use your nose to smell things – 29 **to start
crying** when water begins to come out of your eyes because you are sad

When I came home from school the strange-looking man was there again. He waited at the corner for more than two hours. It's ten o'clock in the evening now and my sister hasn't come home yet. Perhaps the dog has run away and she's looking for it.

I began to write a poem for Sandy:

I love your beautiful green eyes
and your long red hair is nice.

"That's really terrible. I give up for today," I shouted angrily. My sister phoned at lunchtime. She's staying with a friend. The dog is with her. I went to see Arsenal play against Liverpool. It was a good game. Arsenal won 2-1. I'm not a real football fan. I only go there because most of my friends are there.
Wanted to look up Sandy on Facebook. But I can't get that stupid computer going again to get onto the Internet.

I had a nice breakfast with cornflakes, bacon and eggs, toast with marmalade, fruit juice and tea. During the week it's just cornflakes for breakfast, but today I wanted something special. It's a special day today. I've written the first love poem of my life. Here it is:

Dear Sandy. In the sunshine, in the rain,
In cars, on buses, or on a train,
During the day and through the night,
In the dark or in sunlight,
I'll tell you one thing that is true,
The one I'm thinking of is
YOU!

Went to school but it was closed. I forgot that the teachers have
gone on strike for two days. They are asking for more money.
I was sad because I couldn't give my poem to Sandy. What would
she think of it? What does she think of me? What does she think
of the other boys in our class? Perhaps she has already got a
boyfriend. My heart was beating quickly.
In the afternoon I played football in the park with some of the
boys from our neighbourhood. I had to play in goal for most of
the time. I didn't like it much because it was a cold and windy
day and I was freezing. – When I left the park after the match the
strange-looking man was there again.
My stupid sister is still staying with her friend. I hope her friend
likes dogs. Perhaps my sister will stay there, just to keep the dog.
A nice idea.

Tuesday, October 9th

No school today. Brilliant! The teachers are still on strike. They
want more money. – I want more money as well! But my mum

---

13 **to go on strike** to stop working because you are not happy about sth –
20 **neighbourhood** the area where you live – 22 **freezing** very cold – 22 **the match** the
game – 31 **brilliant** excellent, really good

doesn't want to give me any more pocket money. Perhaps I'll get a job as a newspaper boy. But then I would have to get up at six o'clock in the morning. Oh, well!

Wednesday, October 10th

Everything is back to normal. Before school I put my poem into the nicest envelope I could find. Later at school I waited for a chance to give the poem to Sandy. But I couldn't find the right moment. It was only after the last lesson when everybody was leaving the classroom that I was able to do it. In the corridor I walked right behind Sandy and then I put the envelope into her bag. I hope she'll find it there.

When I came home my sister was already there. That stupid dog was lying on my bed. I gave it a kick. My sister shouted at me, "Stop that! If you can get a guitar for Christmas I have the right to keep a dog." Then my mother came in. First she looked at me, then she looked at the dog and in the end she turned to my sister and said, "Wait until your father comes home. You know that I hate dogs." Then she left for Bingo.

It's late at night. I'm thinking of Sandy. Has she read my poem? What does she think of it?

1 **pocket money** money you get from your parents – 9 **envelope** paper case you put a letter in before sending it – 12 **corridor** long space in a building with rooms on both sides

We had a terrible night. I had only just fallen asleep when we were woken up by the fire-brigade. I think it was about 2 am. Our neighbours' house was on fire. There was a lot of smoke. A girl was crying. I couldn't see her. Then I saw Mr Miller, our neighbour, who was standing on the grass in front of his house. He shouted, "There she is!" – "Where?" Mrs Miller asked. "Look, there on the roof." – Judy, Mr and Mrs Miller's daughter, had climbed out of the window and onto the roof. An ambulance arrived and stopped in front of our house. A fireman climbed up a ladder to the roof of the house. He took the girl and carried her down to the ambulance. The ambulance drove away quickly. The firemen were able to put out the fire in about half an hour. At 3 am it was all over and we could go back to sleep.

At school I was very tired. I couldn't follow the lessons. Sandy didn't look at me once. I don't know whether she has read my poem or not.

Kevin and I had a little fight at lunchtime. I think he's in love with Sandy, too. Brian was standing in the corner. He was watching us and he was laughing loudly.

Keep your hands off Sandy or I'll hit you.

Found a note under my desk at school. It said, "Keep your hands off Sandy or I'll hit you." That was all. No name. Nothing. I think Kevin wrote the note.

---

4 **fire-brigade** people who control and stop fire – 5 **smoke** when sth burns you can see fire and smoke – 9 **roof** the top of a house or building, outside

I went to a music shop after school and had a look at all the instruments. I think a keyboard will be better than a guitar. As a keyboard player it might be easier to become a pop star.

With a keyboard and a computer you can easily make your own music. So perhaps I can also get some good software for my computer and then I'll start with the pop business. Wow!! Oh, I forgot. My computer is still broken. Somebody will have to fix it first.

Today the strange-looking man was there again. At 5 pm he met another man in a black Jaguar. They sat in the car and talked to each other. Twenty minutes later the other man got out of the car and went away. The strange-looking man waited in the car for a moment and then he drove away.

Saturday, October 13th

Wanted to see the Arsenal match against Chelsea. But my mum said that she wouldn't give me any more money if I wanted a guitar for Christmas. I told her that I had changed my mind and that I didn't want a guitar any more. After she had given me the money for the match I told her that I wanted a keyboard. Before she could throw things at me I quickly rushed out of the house. I went round to Stephen's and we watched some music videos. Stephen likes British rap music – very loud! I prefer American rap music but I don't like that very much either.

---

15 **Jaguar** type of expensive car – 25 **to change your mind** to make a different plan or have a different opinion – 28 **to rush** to move fast

We were just watching an exciting new rap video when Stephen's
mum came in and shouted, "What the hell is that? Stop that noise!!"
Stephen became angry and shouted back, "It's not too loud.
It's only because you don't like this kind of music. You only
like Madonna and Sting." "Yeah," I said, "I played frisbee with a
Madonna CD yesterday. That's what they are good for." Stephen's
mother didn't know what to say. She closed the door and went
away. Ten minutes later we heard a strange noise. It came from
the lounge. Stephen's mother had put on the
vacuum-cleaner. Stephen switched off the TV and
wanted to show me a new computer game, but I had
to leave because of the football match.

The match was not too bad. But after the game I fell
down the stairs and almost broke my nose. Now my
nose is swollen.

> Sunday, October 14th

Woke up with a headache. I went to the bathroom and had a look
in the mirror. It was terrible. My nose was red and blue and it was
very big.
I didn't go out today. I stayed in the lounge all day long and
watched TV.

> Monday, October 15th

Wanted to stay at home but my mother didn't want to write a
note for school. My nose looked even worse. It had turned blue
and green. I looked like a monster.

---

5 **frisbee** game throwing and catching a disc – 10 **vacuum cleaner** machine to clean
carpets – 12 **football match** football game – 15 **swollen** bigger than normal

At school it was terrible. Everybody was laughing. Even our Geography teacher. At lunch break Sandy came up to me and said that she felt sorry for me. That made my day.

I'm quite happy now. There is still hope for a happy ending to this story.

> Why hasn't Alan's mum got her makeup on yet?

> Why didn't Alan sleep very well?

Think about it...

If you found a dog, would your parents let you keep it?

What are the hard things about having a dog?

---

3 **That made my day** That made me very happy

Went to the shops down at Wood Green. I wanted to buy a
present for Sandy, but I had no idea what to buy. I walked around
for over two hours. It really drove me crazy. In the end I had a
hamburger with chips and went back to the underground station.
Back home I saw the strange-looking man again. He was wearing
a funny old beige raincoat and a black cap. I must find out why
he's waiting at the corner almost every day.
My mum has gone out again. She goes out almost every
evening. I don't know where she's going and she doesn't want to
tell me.

Sandy told me that she liked my poem. At last!!!!!!
I asked her if she would like to sit next to me during lessons. She
said that she wanted to sit next to Kevin because he's very good at
most subjects.
When I came home my sister was crying. The dog had been run
over by a London transport bus. The dog had to be taken to the
vet's. The vet had to operate on the dog and it's not yet clear
whether the dog will live.

My dad phoned this morning. He'll be coming home for a few
days next week. I'm looking forward to that. I'll ask him about his
work on the oil rig. Perhaps one day I can work there, too, and
earn a lot of money.

---

8 **cap** flat type of hat – 21 **to run over** to hit sth with a car – 23 **vet** animal doctor –
23 **to operate on** to cut sth open to fix it – 30 **to look forward to** to be excited about

Kevin is having a party on Saturday. I don't know whether Sandy will be there, too. So I must go to the party and find out.

Friday, October 19th

Sad news from the vet. The dog is dead. My sister stayed in her room all day long and cried her eyes out. Tomorrow is Kevin's party and I still don't know what to wear. What kind of clothes does Sandy like???

Saturday, October 20th

No time for the diary today. I must get ready for the party. It's important.

Sunday, October 21st

I'm sad. Sandy wasn't there. In fact there were no girls at all. There were only Kevin and his Arsenal supporters. Kevin's parents were away for the evening. They had gone out to see a new musical in the Westend. The party was boring – I left at half past nine. – Must try to get Sandy's phone number. She has a little red mobile. Really cool.

Monday, October 22nd

During morning break some of the girls were standing together with Brian. They were looking at a photo on Brian's mobile. It was a photo of Theo Walcott, the England striker. The girls love him.

---

24 **Westend** part of London with lots of theatres – 32 **striker** football postion at the front, a striker is good at scoring goals

Back home I saw the strange-looking man
again. This time he was sitting on a park
bench talking to a good-looking woman
for more than an hour. He must be a spy or
something. I was just passing by when he got
on a bus. So I jumped on as well. I wanted
to find out where he was going. He got off at
Turnpike Lane tube station and went down
the High Road towards Wood Green. He was
walking fast and I could hardly follow him.
Suddenly I noticed something behind a shop
window. I couldn't believe my eyes. It was

my mother. She was cleaning the floors. Now I knew where she
went almost every night. I walked on but the strange-looking
man wasn't there anymore. So I took the next bus home. – I hope
my mum didn't see me. She told me not to walk around North
London after dark. It can be dangerous.

Tuesday, October 23rd

Brian invited Sandy to go to a football match at Spurs', but Sandy
said "No". – Why did she do that? Maybe she's not interested in
football. I only hope that she's not interested in Brian.

Wednesday, October 24th

My dad arrived in the afternoon. He had grown a beard and
looked a bit like Father Christmas. He asked me questions about
school. I didn't tell him that I was in love with Sandy.

---

3 **bench** long seat for a few people – 3 **good-looking** attractive – 5 **spy** sb whose job it is
to watch others in secret – 21 **Spurs** English football team – 28 **beard** when a lot of hair
grows on your face you have a beard

I asked him what life was like on the oil rig. He said, "Well, it's not funny. We sometimes work sixteen hours a day. The weather is bad most of the time and I have to work outside quite often. The people on the oil rig aren't very friendly. They are only there for the money. The only good thing is the food."

Thursday, October 25th

Mum and Dad went out in the late afternoon. So I had the lounge all to myself. I wanted to watch the telly but there was nothing on. So I looked out of the window instead and what did I see? The strange-looking man was talking to two other men who also looked very strange.
I decided to find out about those men. I went outside and followed them into the park. The men were walking towards the lake. When I got there I couldn't see them anymore. "Where are they?" I asked myself. – As it was almost dark outside I couldn't see much.
I walked around the park for about ten minutes.
I almost wanted to give up when I heard a noise right behind me. I turned round and looked straight into the face of a man.
It was the strange-looking man ...

Why doesn't Sandy want to sit next to Alan?

How good was the party?

---

11 **telly** informal word for television – 21 **noise** sound

Think about it...

Is it a good idea to sit next to your best friends in class?

Sandy possibly wants to copy Kevin's answers. Do you think that's OK?

Part II

I think it's about time I gave you some more information about the people in this diary.

My mother

Name	Jane
Age	35
Job	housewife, part-time cleaning lady
Hobbies	Bingo, Sudoko, watching telly
Height	168 cm
Weight	66 kilos
Hair	brown
Eyes	brown

My father

Name	James (Jim for short)
Age	38
Job	electrician
Height	Dad says "seven feet and two inches", but this can't be true
Weight	about 90 kilos

6 **it's about time** I should, I need to – 13 **part-time** working for less than 100% – 30 **feet** approximately 30 cm – 30 **inch** approximately 2.5cm

Hobbies	cricket (in summer), reading the Sunday paper (in winter)
Hair	not much left
Eyes	blue

My sister

Name	Susan (Susie for short)
Age	17 and a half
Job	wants to become a secretary
Height	170 cm
Weight	top secret
Eyes	greenish brown
Hair	changes every week, pink just now
Hobbies	animals, riding horses (but she hasn't got a horse)

Sandy

Name	Sandra Alice Cooper
Age	14
Height	168 cm
Weight	about 55 kilos
Eyes	I dare not look
Hair	long, red

---

30 **I dare not look** I afraid to look

Hobbies	reading music magazines, dancing, listening to all kinds of music
Favourite food	chicken wraps, chocolate muffins

Brian

Name	Brian James Coldwell
Age	15
Height	173 cm
Weight	over 80 kilos. FAT!!!!
Hair	black
Eyes	very small
Hobbies	football
Favourite food	burgers, pakoras

Kevin

Name	Kevin Smith
Age	14 3/4
Height	166 cm
Weight	less than 60 kilos (THIN)
Hair	dirty blond
Eyes	I don't know what colour

19 **pakora** Indian dish often made with vegetables and chicken

Hobbies	computer games
Favourite food	fish and chips

The strange-looking man

Name	I call him "Sherlock Holmes".
Age	about 45
Height	taller than Brian, but not as tall as my father
Weight	not more than 70 kilos
Hair	you can't see his hair because he always wears a cap
Eyes	blue (I think)
Clothes	he always wears an old beige raincoat
Hobbies	hanging around our street
Job	?????

Friday, November 16th

My mother allowed me to watch television all evening. I forgot the diary. Sorry!

Saturday, November 17th

My mother, my sister and I went shopping in Wood Green. My sister bought a pink top. I got some new shoes which I don't like at all. My mother looked at all kinds of things, but didn't buy anything.

---

16 **beige** light brown colour – 16 **raincoat** coat that stops you getting wet

The weather was very bad. It rained all day. My mother told me
to tidy up my room. I found some old photos. My parents really
looked good when they were young. My dad even had lots of hair
then, too.

I also found a piece of paper. It was a page from my diary which I
had thrown away angrily. It said:

Oct 25th: … The strange-looking man looked at me and said,
"What are you doing here? It's too late for a little boy like you to
be running around the park in the evening," I didn't know what
to say; so I ran away. I ran straight home and went to my room.
"Little boy!" that man had said. I'm not a little boy. I'm almost 15
(in words: FIFTEEN!).

Too much homework today. No time for the diary.

My dad is back on holiday. He doesn't want to work on the oil rig
any more. He says it's too boring, too lonely and too dangerous.
He will try to find another job near London.

My sister said, "We don't even know where you are working at the
moment. We only know that it's an oil rig in the North Sea. And
now you want to work in another place?" "Shut up, Susie," Dad
said. "Susie is right," I said, "Where is that oil rig you're working
on?" "Well," Dad said, "it is in the Brent oil field north-east of
Scotland, if you know where that is. And now leave me alone."

4 **to tidy up** to put things back in the right place – 25 **lonely** feeling that you need people,
but nobody is there

34

Sandy wore lipstick today. I wonder why she did that? School was
boring. Too much homework again.
After dinner my father and I sat in my room. He looked at all the
pictures of different pop stars on the wall. Then he asked me, "Do
you have a girlfriend?"
I said, "I don't know yet. Perhaps I'll have one soon."
I asked my dad how he got to know Mum. He said that he had
met her at the school dance. Suddenly my mother came in and
started to laugh. "I remember," she said. "I had to ask you to
dance with me. You were too shy." "Yes, I know," my father said, "I
didn't want to dance at all. But it wasn't so bad."

I didn't go to school this morning. I had to go to
the dentist. He gave me two fillings. Ow! Perhaps I
shouldn't eat so many sweets.
When I went back to school at lunchtime I saw
Kevin in the toilet. He was smoking. I know Sandy
hates people who smoke. If Sandy finds out that Kevin smokes,
he'll be out of the race for Sandy.

Did quite well in the French test. Perhaps I'm starting to like
French after all. I stood behind the kitchen door and listened to
what Mum and Dad were saying:
Mum: When do you go back to work, Jim?

---

3 **lipstick** makeup for your lips – 10 **school dance** party at school – 12 **shy** introvert,
quiet – 19 **dentist** doctor who looks after your teeth – 19 **filling** what dentists put in a
tooth to fix it – 24 **to be out of the race** to not be in the competition any more

Dad:	On Sunday evening. I'll take the night train to Aberdeen and in the morning I'll fly over to the oil rig.
Mum:	Will it be the last time that you have to go back?
Dad:	I hope so. If I get that job in Norwich, I'll never go back to the oil rig again.
Mum:	Do you think the kids and I should move to Norwich, too?
Dad:	That wouldn't be a bad idea. We could at least be together all the time.

Saturday, November 24th

I didn't sleep at all last night. NORWICH! Oh no ... I hope my dad doesn't get the job there. That would be the end.

Sunday, November 25th

A lovely sunny day. Probably the last sunny day of the year. I went jogging in Clissold Park. Later I sat on a park bench where I met "Sherlock Holmes".

Sherlock:	Hi, kid.
Me:	Hello.
Sherlock:	Haven't I seen you before?
Me:	Yes. – You called me a "little boy," but I'm almost 15.
Sherlock	(laughed): I can see that. Tell me, why were you following me the last time I saw you?
Me:	Well, I wanted to find out who you were.
Sherlock:	OK. I'll tell you. I'm a police inspector and we are looking for some drug dealers.
Me:	Have you found them yet?
Sherlock:	No.

That was all the police inspector said. – Then he went away.

---

19 **jogging** slow running – 30 **drug dealer** sb who wells drugs

Worked hard for the Maths test. I'm sure Sandy will like me if I'm good at Maths.
Brian wore a football T-shirt under his school uniform. He was sent home and had to put his normal shirt and tie on.
When I saw Sandy I couldn't believe my eyes. What had happened to her? She looked strange. Then I noticed. Her hair, – her beautiful long red hair, – it wasn't there anymore. Now her hair was very short. Oh no!

I went to school early. Sandy was there, too. I told her I had met a police inspector who was looking for some drug dealers.

Me: Do you think anybody takes drugs at our school?
Sandy: I don't know.
Me: I saw a film about drugs on television the other night. It was terrible.
Sandy: My sister is 21 and she once had a boyfriend who took drugs. It was so sad. One day they had to take him to hospital. A few weeks later he died.
Me: It's terrible that young people die just because drug dealers want to make a lot of money.

Mr Roberts, our Geography teacher, has given us some really stupid homework. For the next four weeks we'll have to look at the moon every night and find out what it looks like. It's really

---

6 **tie** sth you can wear around your neck, usually on top of a shirt

stupid because it'll be cloudy the whole time and you won't be able to see the moon anyway.

Thursday, November 29th

During Assembly the headmaster said that this year's school disco will be held on Friday, December 14th.

Friday, November 30th

The girls were talking about the school disco for most of the day. The boys didn't really know what to say. Most of them hate dancing.

Why doesn't Alan think that he should be called "little boy"?

Why doesn't Alan's dad want to work on the oil rig?

Think about it...

Do you have any of the same hobbies as Alan and his friends and family?

What do you like doing in your free time?

---

1 **cloudy** when the sky is grey and there are clouds in the sky – 7 **Assembly** daily or weekly meeting of teachers and pupils at school

Saturday, December 1st

Met "Sherlock Holmes" in the street outside our school.

Me: Any news from the drug dealers?

Sherlock: No. But you can keep your eyes open and tell me if
     you see anything.

Wow! I'm not "little boy" any more. Now I'm Sherlock's assistant.
Just call me Dr Watson.

Sunday, December 2nd

A rainy day. In the afternoon I lay on my bed and dreamed about
the future.

23 DAYS TILL CHRISTMAS!!! Will I get the keyboard? Will I
be able to become a pop star? If I were a pop star I could get any
girl I wanted ...

Monday, December 3rd

A letter from a company in Norwich arrived today. What will it
say??? I don't want to live in Norwich.

I want to stay in London. All my friends are here and, of course,

Tuesday, December 4th

Haven't found anybody yet who is taking drugs at our school.
Perhaps I'm just too blind to see it. Sandy hasn't been of much
help either. She and all the other girls in my form are only talking
about the school disco.

---

31 **blind** can't see

39

Saw two young men in jeans and leather jackets outside the
school. They were talking to some older pupils. Perhaps they're
selling drugs. I'll find out about it ...
Brian had his hair cut: very short at the back and at the sides, like
Theo Walcott. He looks like a bulldog now.

Great news! I finally got Sandy's phone
number. – Mum and Dad came home
with a big parcel today. I hope that it's my
Christmas present (the keyboard)!
Dad wasn't very happy. He only has a free
weekend and must return to the oil rig on

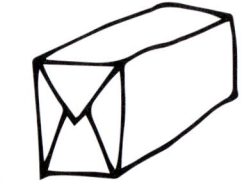

Monday – yet again. The company in Norwich won't decide
about his job before the beginning of January. So that gives me
a little bit of time.

Sandy was very quiet today. At lunchtime I saw the reason why.
She had been to the dentist. Now she's wearing a brace on her
teeth. I didn't know what to say. I'm also not sure what I think
of it.
Kevin is wearing an earring in his left ear. Ugh!! During the
French lesson I had to read aloud. My voice sounded funny. I
think it's finally breaking – at last! I'm finally becoming a MAN!!!!

---

3 **leather** material made from animal skin – 14 **parcel** package – 26 **brace** sth metal
dentists put on your teeth to make them grow in the correct position – 30 **voice** sound
that comes out of your mouth when you speak – 31 **finally breaking** when a boy's voice
becomes low

Wrote the first song of my life:

1. Is it difficult to be young?
   Will this little song ever be sung?
   Will I be rich or will I be poor?
   I'll never live in Norwich, that's for sure.
2. Will I travel 'round the world?
   Will I find a beautiful girl?
   Will I ever be a man,
   or will I just be a football fan?

Chorus: I have many questions. Who gives me the answers?

I've tried to sing the song all afternoon, but it's very hard for me because my voice only makes funny noises.

Sunday, December 9th

Read an article in the Sunday Mirror:
Police inspector hurt in gun battle with drug dealers.
There was also a photo showing a police inspector in an ambulance. He looked a lot like "Sherlock Holmes" ...

Monday, December 10th

Spoke to Sandy about Sherlock. I didn't say much because my voice keeps breaking all the time. Sandy didn't say much either. I think she's having problems with her brace.

Tuesday, December 11th

My sister is growing up, too. This time she didn't bring a dog home – this time it was her new boyfriend. My mother says that he's much too old for her. But I think he only looks about nineteen or so. He's got very short black hair, big ears and a small nose. I wonder where Susie found him?

Wednesday, December 12th

Steve (Susie's boyfriend) was here again. I hope he doesn't stay any longer than the dog did. At least he doesn't bark at night.

---

8 **hurt** injured, shot – 8 **gun battle** fight between people using guns

Tried to phone Sandy, but she didn't answer the phone. I wonder
why? – School disco tomorrow. Will it be an important day in my
life? Just think of my parents!!

Brian wasn't at school today. I hope he's ill and can't come to the
disco. I went home straight after school and had a little rest on
the sofa. I didn't feel very well.
School disco started at 7 pm. I couldn't see Brian. Thank God.
Kevin had another ring in his left ear. What does he need two
rings in his ear for? One ring is ugly enough!
Sandy arrived five minutes after I did. She looked great in her
new black jeans, leather boots and a green sweatshirt.
She talked to the French teacher for quite a long time. Then she
went to dance with some of the girls from our form. I stood by
the wall most of the time and watched Sandy. She didn't look at
me once.
After the disco I saw Sandy standing at the bus stop. "Where
have you been all evening?" she asked. "Oh, around," I answered.
I didn't know what else to say. We stood there waiting for more
than 20 minutes, but no bus turned up. "I think we've missed the
last bus. Let's walk, shall we?" said Sandy. "Can I walk you home?"
I asked. "That would be great," she said.
We didn't talk much on the way to Sandy's house. When we
arrived there I wanted to kiss her but I was too nervous. I just
said "See you on Monday," turned around and started to leave.
Then Sandy said, "I'm going to the cinema next week. Would you
like to come with me?" "Wow, I'd love to," I shouted. "See you!"
Then I ran off.

15 **ugly** not attractive – 25 **to turn up** to arrive

Saturday, December 15th

Oh, what a happy day!!!!!!!!!!!

Sunday, December 16th

Watched Manchester United against Arsenal on TV. Not a good
match. No goals.

Monday, December 17th

Dad phoned up. He doesn't want to stay on the oil rig any longer.
There was a terrible storm and he was frightened. I'm a bit
worried about him, too. He's not a very good swimmer.
Sandy told me that she wanted to go to the cinema on Wednesday
at 6 pm, if that would be all right with me. I'd go any time or
anywhere, if she asked me!

Tuesday, December 18th

While I was doing my homework, I could hear Susie and my
mother in the lounge. They were talking about problems. I
could only understand that it was about Susie's boyfriend and
drugs. This could be important. Perhaps I can find out more
about it ...

Wednesday, December 19th

Went to the cinema with Sandy. It was wonderful.

Thursday, December 20th

I think I'm in love for the first time in my life. What a feeling! Life
is great!

Friday, December 21st

Last day of school before Christmas. Sad news for me. Sandy
told me that she would go to Scotland with her parents over
Christmas. So I won't be able to see her for the next two weeks.
Perhaps I should write another song, this time about love and
loneliness.

Saturday, December 22nd

Stayed in bed until 12 o'clock. I don't know whether I'm happy or
sad.
Dad came home. He's not going back to the oil rig. Mum arrived
with another big parcel. Susie's boyfriend was arrested by the police.

Sunday, December 23rd

A quiet day. Nothing happened.

Monday, December 24th

I woke up at 5 o'clock in the morning. A lot of questions came to
my mind:

---

13 **loneliness** the feeling of being on your own – 18 **whether** if – 31 **to come to your
mind** to think of sth

Will Sandy be my girlfriend?
What will Brian do?
Will Kevin still be my best friend?
Will our family move to another place when Dad gets a new job?
Will Susie get a new dog or a new boyfriend?
What about the drug dealers?
Will "Sherlock Holmes" get out of hospital soon?
Will I get my keyboard tomorrow?
Will I become a pop star?

All these questions, and tomorrow is

CHRISTMAS!!!

Why is Alan excited about Christmas?

Why didn't Alan walk Sandy home?

Think about it ...

There are a lot of questions in Alan's head at the end of the diary. What kind of questions do you ask yourself about the future?

Activities

Focus on people

1 What does Alan like? And you?

Complete the table with Alan's favourite things. Then, fill in yours.

	Alan	You
school subjects		
hobbies		
pop group		
football team		
interests		
friends		
colour		

2 What does Alan worry about?

Circle 7 things that Alan worries about.

bad food

having a boyfriend/girlfriend

long walk to school

becoming a pop star

making his teacher angry

sleeping a lot

finding sports really difficult

not having enough money

hating maths

getting fat

Focus on grammar

1 Talking about the future

Alan thinks about the future in his diary. Tick these sentences if
the grammar is correct or write the correct sentence if it is wrong.

a. I hope she would be in school tomorrow.

....

b. I'm will go to the cinema next week. Would you like to come
with me?

....

c. Perhaps my sister will stay there, just to keep the dog.

....

d. I think a keyboard is going be better than a guitar.

....

e. He's not going back to the oil rig.

....

f. I don't know whether Sandy won't be there, too.

....

2 *Will* or *going to*?

Write <u>will</u> or <u>going to</u> in the correct box to complete the rules
about when to use them.

_____	• make decision at the time of speaking • state a fact about the future • make a promise • make a prediction • with: I think/ I guess / I hope / probably / possibly
_____	• future event that has been planned before the time of speaking • make a future prediction based on facts

Build your vocabulary

Focus on words and phrases

1 Can you think of the word?

Complete the crossword with words from the story.

1. Girls put it on. 2. Alan tried to write it. 3. You put a letter into it. 4. He gives you fillings. 5. Boots are made of it. 6. A colour. 7. Everybody has it. 8. You can sit on it. 9. The teachers at Alan's school went on it. 10. A person.

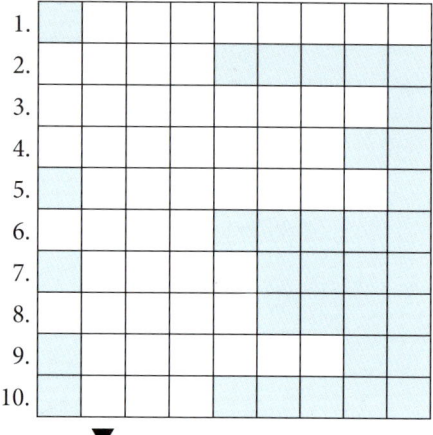

Most people are afraid of it: _____

2 What is it?

Write the word from the story under the picture.

a. _____

b. _____

c. _____

d. _____

e. _____

f. _____

g. _____

h. _____

3 How does the sentence end?

Match the sentences to complete the expressions from the story.

1. I think it's a …

2. I told Sandra to keep her …

3. All of the hospital staff are going to go on …

4. I was going to go to the cinema, but then I changed …

5. The great news that Sam told me has …

6. It's about …

7. What comes to …

a. … your mind when you see this photo?

b. … time you bought some new shoes.

c. … strike about their working hours.

d. … made my day.

e. … my mind and decided to stay at home.

f. … fingers off my brother.

g. … pity that Tom can't come to the party.

1		2		3		4		5		6		7	

Alan Brown's Diary – the mind map

Make your own mind map of words connected to the story.
Think of words to add to each topic area. You can add your own
topic areas too.

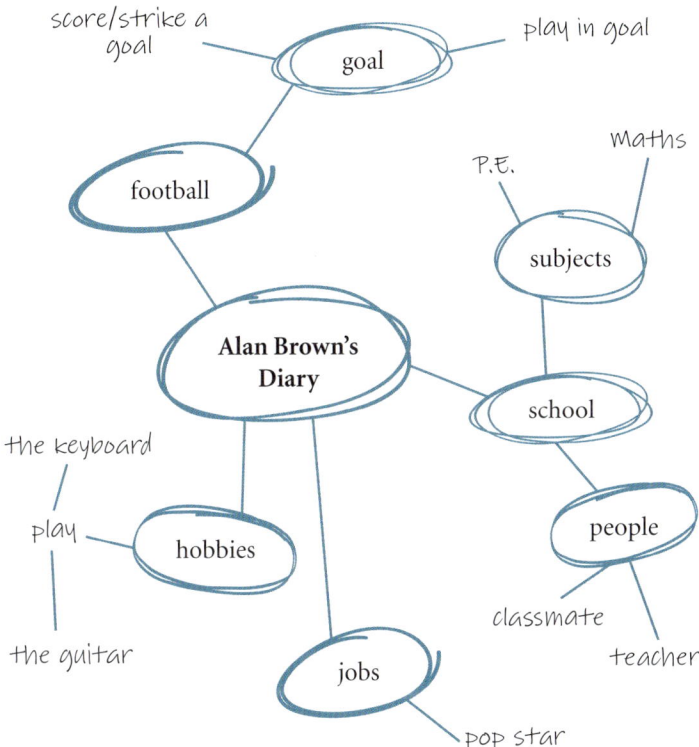

Compare your words with the words in on the next pages. Did
you include some of the same words? Tick the words you know
and look back at the text and explanations to check the meanings
of any new words. You can add your own words and notes to the
glossary like the examples here.

Glossary

	New word?	Notes / connected words
Football		
fan	☐	
game	☐	
goal	☐	
match	☐	
play against	☐	
play in goal	☐	
striker	☐	
supporter	☐	
ticket	☐	
Hobbies		
bingo	☐	
computer games	☐	
football	☐	
horse riding	☐	
music	☐	
play the guitar	☐	
shopping	☐	
Sudoku	☐	Japanese numbers game
watch telly	☐	
write a diary	☐	
Jobs		
dentist	☐	
drug dealer	☐	
housewife	☐	
milkman	☐	
oil rig worker	☐	
police inspector	☐	

	New word?	Notes / connected words
pop star	☐	
vet	☐	
words	☐	

School

	New word?	Notes / connected words
assembly	☐	
class	☐	
corridor	☐	
desk	☐	
headmaster/mistress	☐	
holiday	☐	
homework	☐	
learn vocabulary	☐	
lesson	☐	
lunchtime	☐	
physical education	☐	
school cafeteria	☐	
school dance / disco	☐	
school uniform	☐	
subject	☐	
teacher	☐	

Find out more

1. Why do people write diaries? Find 10 reasons why and make a list here.

10 Reasons why people write diaries

1. _____
2. _____
3. _____
4. _____
5. _____
6. _____
7. _____
8. _____
9. _____
10. _____

2. Find out what the most popular topics are that people your age write about.

3. Try it out. Write your own diary for a week and then decide if you want to carry on.

Monday	
Tuesday	
Wednesday	
Thursday	
Friday	
Saturday	
Sunday	

Answer key

Focus on the story – questions at the end of each section

Part 1 September
- On an oil rig off the coast of Scotland.
- Because he keeps thinking about Sandy.

Part 1 1st – 15th October
- She's crying because she is worried about Alan's dad.
- The dog kept barking.

Part 1 16th – 31st October
- Because Kevin is very good at most subjects.
- Not good. There were no girls there. Alan was very disappointed that Sandy wasn't there.

Part 2 November
- Because he is 15 years old.
- Because it's boring and dangerous.

Part 2 December
- Because he's hoping to get the keyboard so that he can become a pop star.
- Because he was too nervous.

Focus on the people

1. (for Alan): 1. Physical Education, Music, 2. football, pop music, 3. –, 4. Arsenal, 5. Girls, 6. Sandy, Kevin, Stephen, 7. Red

2. have a boyfriend/girlfriend, become a pop star, sleep a lot, don't have enough money, hate maths, parent is away from home a lot, an annoying brother or sister

Focus on grammar

1. a. I hope she will be in school tomorrow.
   b. I'm going to the cinema next week. Would you like to come with me?
   c. Correct.
   d. I think a keyboard will be better than a guitar.
   e. Correct.
   f. I don't know whether Sandy will be there, too.

2. will / going to

Focus on words and phrases

1.

1.	L	I	P	S	T	I	C	K
2.	P	O	E	M				
3.	E	N	V	E	L	O	P	E
4.	D	E	N	T	I	S	T	
5.		L	E	A	T	H	E	R
6.	P	I	N	K				
7.		N	A	M	E			
8.	B	E	N	C	H			
9.		S	T	R	I	K	E	
10.	S	P	Y					

2. a. oil rig, b. envelope, c. glasses, d. bench, e. sweatshirt, f. insect, g. lipstick, h. tie

3. 1. g 2. f 3. c 4. c 5. 6. b 7. a

Photos:

6 Shutterstock (GoodStudio), New York; **9,16,17,26,30,31,32,33** Shutterstock (Fosin), New York; **9** Shutterstock (muuraa), New York; **Cover U1** Shutterstock (SnowStock), New York; **Various** Shutterstock (olnik_y), New York; **9,49** Shutterstock (leungchopan), New York; **11** Shutterstock (Dirtymono), New York; **12** Shutterstock (Om Yos), New York; **15** Shutterstock (MicroOne), New York; **15** Shutterstock (NaDo_Krasivo), New York; **16** Shutterstock (Eric Isselee), New York; **17** Shutterstock (valeriiaarnaud), New York; **19** Shutterstock (Matanat Babayeva), New York; **21** Shutterstock (ArtMari), New York; **22** Shutterstock (Evgeniy Yatskov), New York; **25** Shutterstock (anfisa focusova), New York; **26** Shutterstock (katatonia82), New York; **26** Shutterstock (Andrey Mertsalov), New York; **30** Shutterstock (Syda Productions), New York; **30** Shutterstock (Markus Gann), New York; **31** Getty Images (Cookie Studio), München; **31** Shutterstock (Rehan Qureshi), New York; **32** Shutterstock (Solphoto), New York; **32** Shutterstock (PT Images), New York; **33** Shutterstock (Nbenbow), New York; **33** Shutterstock (joppo), New York; **35** Shutterstock (Kseniya Art), New York; **40** Shutterstock (Aine), New York; **47** Shutterstock (Roman Ar), New York; **53.1** Shutterstock (Nerthuz), New York; **53.2** Shutterstock (buteo), New York; **53.3** Shutterstock (Jaengpeng), New York; **53.4** Shutterstock (Yuriy Boyko), New York; **53.5** Shutterstock (kustomer), New York; **53.6** Shutterstock (cynoclub), New York; **53.7** Shutterstock (Neamov), New York; **53.8** Shutterstock (Dragonskydrive), New York; **58** Shutterstock (Martial Red), New York